CONTENTS

INTRODUCTION

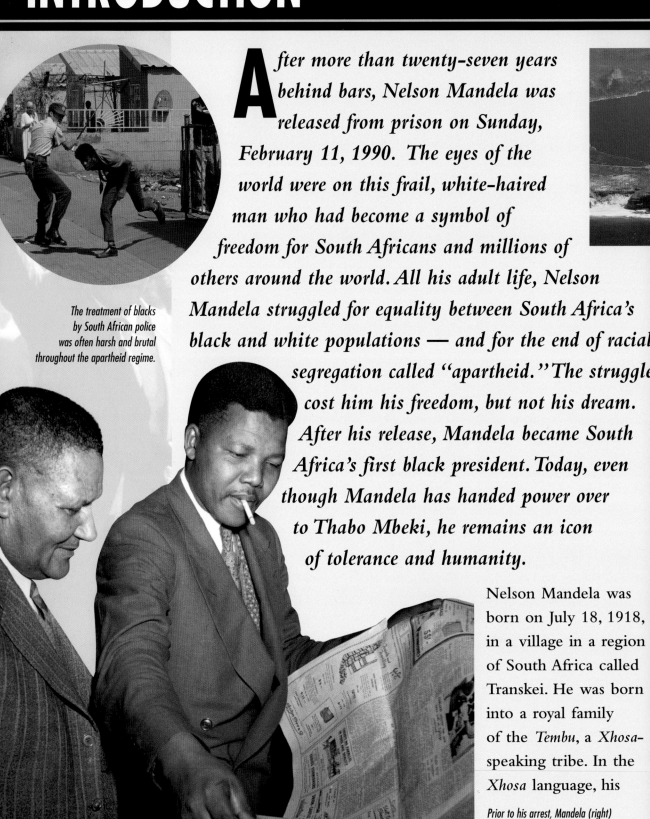

After more than twenty-seven years behind bars, Nelson Mandela was released from prison on Sunday, February 11, 1990. The eyes of the world were on this frail, white-haired man who had become a symbol of freedom for South Africans and millions of others around the world. All his adult life, Nelson Mandela struggled for equality between South Africa's black and white populations — and for the end of racial segregation called "apartheid." The struggle cost him his freedom, but not his dream. After his release, Mandela became South Africa's first black president. Today, even though Mandela has handed power over to Thabo Mbeki, he remains an icon of tolerance and humanity.

The treatment of blacks by South African police was often harsh and brutal throughout the apartheid regime.

Nelson Mandela was born on July 18, 1918, in a village in a region of South Africa called Transkei. He was born into a royal family of the *Tembu*, a *Xhosa*-speaking tribe. In the *Xhosa* language, his

Prior to his arrest, Mandela (right) was a prominent lawyer in Johannesburg, South Africa.

Congress Youth League. By 1948, the Youth League dominated the ANC, and in 1950, Mandela became its president.

he beautiful South African countryside (above) was scarred y decades of civil unrest during the twentieth century.

irth name, *Rolihlahla*, means "stirring up trouble." Mandela vas educated at Fort Hare University, from which e was expelled in 1940. He returned home, but ran way to Johannesburg to void an arranged marriage. He eventually obtained law degree from the University of South Africa. With the assistance of Walter Sisulu, Mandela and his friend, Oliver Tambo, set up South Africa's first black law firm. n 1944, frustrated that the African National Congress ANC) had little effect on the vhite government, the group ormed the African National

Even after retirement, Nelson Mandela remains an influential figure in world affairs.

INTRODUCTION

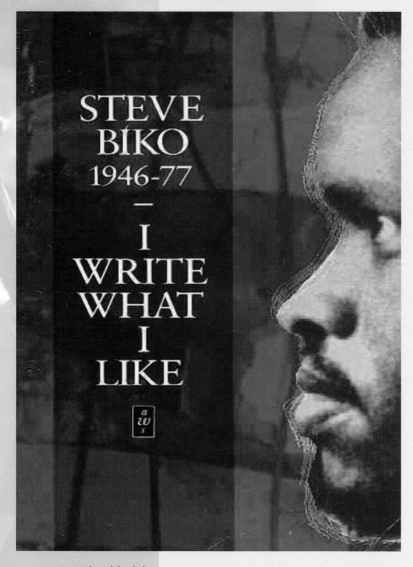

STEVE
BIKO
1946-77
–
I
WRITE
WHAT
I
LIKE

Steve Biko and the Black Consciousness movement struggled against apartheid in the 1970s.

> "In my country we go to prison first and then become President."
>
> *Nelson Mandela*

During Mandela's prison term, his supporters continued the struggle on his behalf. In the 1970s, the Black Consciousness movement — led by Steve Biko — took up the cause, urging blacks to have pride in their own identity. Then, in the 1980s, the United Democratic Front (UDF) launched a national campaign called "Release Mandela." With an outbreak of shocking violence in the 1980s, and the election of President F. W. de Klerk, the political leadership in South Africa also realized that things would have to change.

The South African government banned the ANC after the Sharpeville Massacre in 1961, in which police shot sixty-nine protesters. This incident turned Mandela away from peaceful protest to more aggressive methods of opposition. In 1964, he was sentenced to life in prison for sabotage and treason.

By the end of the decade, the South African government began negotiating his release, with Mandela himself determining the terms of his freedom. On February 11, 1990, cheering crowds greeted Nelson Mandela — a free man once again.

Mandela's release marked the beginning of a new chapter for South Africa. When de Klerk announced that the government planned to phase out apartheid gradually, Mandela realized the impatience of the South African people and forced de Klerk to increase the pace of change. In 1994, the first universal elections were held, and Mandela was elected as the first black president of South Africa. Nelson Mandela retired in 1999, but he still plays an active role in the affairs of his country. And while his country still faces many challenges, South African will always remember the role Mandela played in destroying the hated system of apartheid.

South Africa lies at the south end of the African continent. Rich in gold and diamonds, the country was of great importance to white settlers in the nineteenth and twentieth centuries.

Nelson Mandela has been married three times, and has forty-five children and grandchildren.

The Dutch were among the first Europeans to arrive in South Africa. The Dutch East India Trading Company (center) used its fine fleet to transport goods in and out of Africa.

This Bantu boy is learning traditional hunting techniques. The Bantus have lived in South Africa for hundreds of years.

South Africa is a country with a troubled history. Ever since the first Europeans, the Dutch and British, arrived in the fifteenth century, they fought to control this vast land and created a society in which — for most of the twentieth century — a white minority ruled South Africa. Nelson Mandela and many others challenged South Africa's long tradition of assumed racial superiority by whites over blacks.

Earliest inhabitants

Nomadic hunters and gatherers first inhabited the southern tip of Africa, and before the seventeenth century, various *Bantu*-speaking peoples moved into the region, including *Sotho, Swazi, Xhosa* (Mandela's people) and *Zulu*.

In 1488, Portuguese explorer Bartholomeu Diaz became the first European to sail around the tip of South Africa. Dutch and Huguenot settlers, known as "*Boers*" (which means farmers), arrived in the seventeenth century. They took land from the native population. The British followed in the nineteenth century. Resentment quickly grew between the Europeans and the native peoples.

Battle for gold

Diamonds were discovered in South Africa in 1867, followed by gold in 1886. These discoveries brought hoard of foreign prospectors, and transformed the country into a landscape of mines and ore dumps. The new arrivals caused conflict with the Boers, and led to Britain's attempt to take control of the Transvaal region in northeast South Africa. Although initially the Boers defeated the British, the Anglo–Boer War of 1899–1902 resulted in the Boers surrendering control of the Transvaal. The British also seized the diamond and gold mines.

BANTUS

Some of the earliest inhabitants of South Africa were the nomadic *Bantus*, or Bushmen. In ancient times, they were the most numerous tribe in the region. Today, only about twenty-six thousand survive — most of whom live in the Kalahari Desert.

AFRIKANERS

Afrikaners (formerly called Boers, meaning farmers) descended from the original Dutch, German, and French settlers. Originally, they spoke Dutch, but as they began to adopt African words into their speech, their language changed, and is now known as *Afrikaans*.

World War II

During World War II (1939–1945), South Africa joined the Allies in fighting against Germany. The war meant that Europe was no longer able to supply South Africa with manufactured goods, so the country made and processed its own supplies. With many whites fighting overseas, large numbers of black workers moved from mining jobs to the new industries in the cities. Mandela became part of this migration when he moved to Johannesburg in 1941.

Founding of the Union

In 1910, the British colonies of the Cape of Good Hope and Natal, and the former Boer republics of the Orange Free State and Transvaal, formed the Union of South Africa. Despite rebellions on the eve of World War I (1914–18), the Union became stronger and even expanded when it seized control of Namibia (then called German Southwest Africa).

The National Party

In 1914, General J. B. M. Herzog founded the National Party to protect and promote *Afrikaner* interests, which he believed were being engulfed by British influence. Herzog was also adamantly opposed to people from different races mixing, initially proposing a "two-stream" policy that would allow Afrikaners and English to develop separate cultures and traditions. When Herzog became prime minister, his plans were implemented, and the *Afrikaans* language was also officially adopted and recognized.

Dutch settlers, led by General J. B. M. Herzog, fought the British during the Boer Wars. The British combated the Boers' guerrilla warfare by rounding up non-combatants and putting them in concentration camps.

Apartheid

In 1948, the Afrikaner National Party gained power under Daniel Malan, and introduced the policy of "*apartheid*" — which means "apartness" in the Afrikaans language. Malan justified it as a "separate but equal" development, despite the fact that only the 4.5-million white minority had any say in the nation's affairs. That left 23 million black people who weren't allowed to vote in parliamentary elections, and who were restricted in their use of most public places and institutions.

Birth of apartheid

Until the twentieth century, British authorities allowed all men — including blacks — who were at least twenty-one and who owned property or had money, to vote. After the Boer War, however, the British began excluding natives from voting, largely to make peace with the Boers, who were fiercely opposed to political rights for Africans.

Inequalities

Under apartheid, Africans, Europeans, and Indians lived in separate areas called "*Bantustans*" or homelands. Selected jobs were reserved for whites. The leaders justified their rulings by promising that Africans would have full rights in their Bantustans. In practice, it meant that Africans had the poorest homes, schools, and hospitals. The school curriculum drawn up for black children was also vastly inferior to that for whites. Finally, the Prohibition of Mixed Marriages Act forbade inter-racial marriage.

Throughout South Africa, signs reminded people where they could or could not go. "Whites only"or "Non-Whites only" signs appeared outside all public places, including transportation terminals, restaurants, and beaches.

STRAND EN SEE
NET BLANKES
BEACH AND SEA
WHITES ONLY

DANIEL *Malan*

The South African politician, Daniel Malan (1874–1959), believed firmly in white supremacy and a society arranged on a class basis. He became prime minister of South Africa in 1948 and initiated the policy of apartheid and the Group Areas Act, which divided the country into White, Black, and Colored zones.

ORIGIN *of apartheid*

The term apartheid was coined in the 1930s by Afrikaner intellectuals who formed the South African Bureau for Racial Affairs (SABRA). The organization called for a policy of separate development of races. SABRA was founded in opposition to the liberal South African Institute of Race Relations.

Pass laws

Every African over sixteen had to carry a passbook whenever they left the Bantustans. This document showed that the bearer had a job in a white-designated area, and therefore needed to travel there. The police had the power to stop Africans and demand their passbook. People not carrying a passbook could be arrested and imprisoned. Africans who did not have a passbook were condemned to live in areas where job opportunities were small and poverty reigned.

Enforced apartness

As a result of the new laws, Africans lived like foreigners in their own country. Ghettos existed in many countries, but never on such an extreme and massive scale, with racial groups physically separated from one another.

Resistance

The African National Congress (ANC) formed in 1912. This multiracial, nationalist organization aimed to extend voting rights to the entire population of South Africa, and to end racial discrimination there. Yet after thirty years of peaceful petitions to the government, the ANC had achieved no concessions.

It would take a new generation of young radicals in the 1940s to plot a more militant (aggressive) course of action. Nelson Mandela was drawn to this new group upon his arrival in Johannesburg.

The old guard

The Christian-educated founders of the ANC were mostly members of the African middle-class — doctors, teachers, or priests. They wanted to extend voting rights from the black middle class to the rest of South Africa. They had no plans to overthrow the white government, and instead put their faith in petitions, pleas, and speeches. However, the two South African prime ministers who dominated political life before 1948, J. C. Smuts and J. B. M. Herzog, were committed segregationists who disregarded all appeals to end apartheid.

Under apartheid, blacks lived apart from whites in poor ghettos. Residents used flimsy materials such as corrogated metal and leftover cement, wood, and windows to build their shelters.

The Youth League

In 1944, a group of radical young Africans, including Nelson Mandela, Oliver Tambo, and Walter Sisulu, formed the ANC Youth League. The Youth League acknowledged the ANC's accomplishments but criticized its weak leadership. The Youth League aimed to organize mass protests and civil disobedience to force the white government to give rights to Africans.

Walter Sisulu, along with Nelson Mandela, was one of the founding members of the ANC Youth League.

Defiance Campaign

In 1952, the ANC began a Defiance Campaign against the government's apartheid laws, aiming to make them unworkable. People tore up or burned their passbooks and marched without them into "whites only" areas. Nelson Mandela, now a member of the National Executive of the ANC, was one of them.

The government began to crack down on the protesters in an increasingly brutal way, and many were arrested, but the protesters were willing to accept imprisonment for their beliefs. The campaig caused the United Nations to pass its first resolutio condemning apartheid.

Freedom Charter

In 1954, a multi-racial group of three thousand people from all the anti-apartheid movements within South Africa met at Kliptown near Johannesburg. This Congress of the People produc the Freedom Charter, which set out the movement objectives for a non-racial, democratic governmen and equality for all before the law. However, the police broke up the Congress and took the names and addresses of many of those present.

Sharpeville

On March 21, 1960, one of the other organization fighting against apartheid, the Pan Africanist Congress (PAC), called for a one-day protest against the pass laws. In Sharpeville, near Johannesburg, a crowd of unarmed demonstrators surrounded the police station. The police opened fire on the crowd, killing sixty-nine people and wounding many more.

WALTER *Sisulu*

Walter Sisulu (1912–2003) was a businessman and local leader in Johannesburg when Nelson Mandela met him in 1941. The two men formed a lifelong friendship. Sisulu joined the ANC in 1940 and in 1949 became its general secretary. He encouraged Mandela to attend meetings of the ANC. Sisulu and Mandela later spent many years in prison together.

MANDELA *marries*

In 1944, Nelson Mandela married his first wife, Evelyn Mase, with whom he had a son, Thembi. That relationship ended, and in 1957, he met Nomzamo Winifred Madikizela whom he married in 1958. She was a social worker who also campaigned for the ANC.

any protesters were shot in the back. The assacre made headlines all around the world. he South African government declared a State of mergency and banned the ANC — which meant at its members could be arrested and imprisoned r up to ten years.

The Trials

uring the 1950s, Mandela was banned from public peaking, confined to Johannesburg, and then rrested and imprisoned. In the latter half of the ecade, he was one of the accused in the epic reason Trials. The Treason Trials collapsed in 1961.

With the ANC now illegal, the government was using every measure it could to suppress opposition to apartheid. The ANC leaders resumed their work from secret headquarters. Mandela emerged as the leading figure in this new phase of political struggle. He gave an electrifying speech at an All African Conference in Pietermaritzburg in March 1961. The purpose of the conference was to decide how to react to the government's banning of the ANC. Mandela argued that a government which ignored the black majority was "not valid," and that his people should do anything necessary to fight for their rights.

> "How can I be expected to believe that this same racial discrimination, which has been the cause of so much injustice and suffering right through the years, should now operate here to give me a fair and open trial? I consider myself neither morally nor legally obliged to obey laws made by a Parliament in which I am not represented. That the will of the people is the basis of the authority of government, is a principle universally acknowledged as sacred throughout the civilized world."

Mandela's defense at the Rivonia Trial

Bodies of dead protesters lay on the streets of Sharpeville.

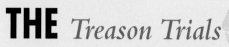

THE *Treason Trials*

The South African government had long tried to imprison the leaders of the ANC and other anti-apartheid organizations. In 1956, the police arrested most of the leaders of the ANC and charged them with treason. The trials lasted for five years, after which every one of the accused was acquitted.

Defendants at the Treason Trials discuss the progress of their case against the government.

Armed struggle

Mandela and others believed that not only should they continue to fight apartheid, but also that they should take up arms against the government. Mandela believed that there were just two choices — submit or fight. In 1961, he formed and led the militant wing of the ANC, "*Umkhhonto we Sizwe*," meaning "Spear of the Nation," with the intention of committing acts of sabotage against government buildings, pass offices, and electric towers.

The Black Pimpernel

this time, Mandela went into hiding from the
lice. He was forced to live apart from his family.
e moved from place to place to avoid detection
government informers and police spies. But he
ll managed to appear at important events,
ten using a disguise as a chauffeur or gardener.
cause Mandela was so successful at evading
e police, the press began to call him the Black
mpernel. He traveled to other countries in West
nd North Africa to motivate support, and also
aveled to England, where he met politicians
nd even made time for some sightseeing.

Arrest

n August 5, 1962, Mandela was arrested while
disguised as a white friend's chauffeur. He was
charged with inciting strikes and with
illegally leaving the country. Throughout
the trial, Mandela conducted his own
defense, and wore traditional African
dress to court. However, despite a
rigorous defense, he was found
guilty and sentenced to five years
imprisonment. Mandela was
sent to prison on Robben
Island, a notoriously
bleak jail on an island
about 7.5 miles
(12 kilometers)
off the coast
of Cape Town.

Rivonia trial

While in prison, Mandela was brought
to court again with all the leaders of
the ANC who were arrested
at Rivonia — their secret
headquarters near Johannesburg.
They were charged with
sabotage and attempting
to overthrow the government,
offenses for which they faced
the death sentence.

*Mandela wore
traditional clothing
during his trial
in 1962.*

Mandela spoke for more than four hours from the
witness box in a now-famous speech. He said that
the ideal of a democratic and free society was
something which he hoped to live for and to
achieve, but, he added, "... if needs be, it is an
ideal for which I am prepared to die." The judge
sentenced the defendants to life imprisonment.

BIRTH *of a republic*

In 1961, South Africa became a republic and withdrew from
the British Commonwealth. Protesting its apartheid polocies,
the United Nations refused to recognize the republic, and
South Africa began a thirty-year period of international
isolation. The country was excluded from international
organizations and sporting events and also had economic
and trade sanctions imposed.

*"All lawful modes
of expressing
opposition to the
principle of white
supremacy had been
closed by legislation,
and we were placed
in a position in
which we had
either to accept
a permanent state
of inferiority or
to defy the
government.
We chose to defy
the government."*

Mandela's defense
at the Rivonia Trial

STRUGGLE AGAINST APARTHEID

During Mandela's imprisonment, the struggle against apartheid continued. Many countries condemned the sentences, and the United Nations called for the unconditional release of the prisoners. The movement was encouraged by the independence of Zimbabwe, Angola, and Mozambique, and by the Black Consciousness movement in South Africa led by Steve Biko. In 1976, the Soweto massacre led to mass strikes and attacks on police stations and government buildings throughout South Africa.

Mandela (left) talks with fellow ANC member Walter Sisulu in the prison compound at Robben Island.

Robben Island

Nelson Mandela and the other Rivonia Trial prisoners were incarcerated in South Africa's harshest prison, Robben Island. The island was freezing cold in winter and scorching hot in summer. They could wear only short trousers and no shoes, and slept on mats on the floor. Mandela's cell was less than 32 square feet (3 square meters), and lit by a single 40-watt lightbulb. He was confined to his cell for sixteen hours every day.

Treatment of prisoners

Prisoners on Robben Island were allowed to receive and send one letter every six months. These were heavily censored and often deliberately not mailed. Officially, prisoners were allowed two visits a year but Mandela saw his wife just three times in five years. He was not even allowed to attend the funerals of his mother or son when they died. Despite these harsh conditions, he remained determined never to let his spirit be broken.

STEVE *Biko*

Steve Biko (1946–77) was a black activist and founder of the Black Consciousness movement. He studied medicine at Natal University, where he first became involved in politics as a student union leader. He was a popular figure, with his encouragement of black self-reliance, but was frequently detained by police. In 1977, he was arrested and died twenty-six days later from brain damage sustained during beatings and neglect at the hands of prison staff. He had never been convicted of any crime.

WINNIE *Mandela*

While Mandela was in prison, his wife Winnie did not cease campaigning. She was repeatedly detained without trial and tortured, jailed, and was also a victim of attempted murder. In 1977, she was put under house arrest in a small village in the right-wing heartland of the Orange Free State. The house had no running water or electricity, and she was confined there under police guard at night, and over weekends and holidays.

Black Consciousness

the 1970s, a new generation of young radicals, aded by Steve Biko, took up the cause that came known as the Black Consciousness ovement. Biko believed that blacks should not dependent upon white society, but rather be vare and proud of their own identity.

Soweto 1976

1976, the government announced that half the hool curriculum for black students would be ught in Afrikaans, the language of the white

minority. Many teachers did not speak this language, and many children did not understand it. Students in Soweto staged a demonstration against this policy in June. It started peacefully, but then the police panicked and started firing. They killed more than five hundred young protesters, many of whom were simply running away. Afterwards, Africans erupted in a fury of anger, attacking police stations and government buildings.

Despite the imprisonment of her husband and the attention of the police, Winnie Mandela remained a high-profile campaigner for the anti-apartheid movement.

The funerals for the victims of the Soweto massacre were highly emotional events.

17

STRUGGLE AGAINST APARTHEID

"Release Mandela"

The government hoped that the prisoners on Robben Island would be forgotten, but the anti-apartheid movement continued to fight for their release. In fact, the movement to free Mandela went global, with the United Nations calling for his release and demonstrations held around the world. Many countries imposed trade and sporting sanctions, leaving South Africa increasingly isolated. Nelson Mandela had become the most famous political prisoner in the world.

P. W. Botha served as prime minister of South Africa until 1989.

Total Strategy

In 1978, P. W. Botha became prime minister of South Africa and introduced his Total Strategy — a plan of action designed to solve the country's problems. He hoped it would appease both whites and blacks. Even though his plan relaxed some of the laws restricting blacks, it gave greater powers to the security forces. Botha aimed to reform the system rather than replace it, so the protests continued.

International sanctions

In order to put additional pressure on the government, the ANC and the unions campaigned for foreign companies to stop investing in South Africa and for countries to boycott South African goods.

P. W. *Botha*

The South African political leader, Pieter Willem Botha, was born in 1916 and became prime minister in 1978. Botha initiated some limited reforms of apartheid policies and began negotiations with Nelson Mandela, but he also harshly repressed dissent.

A large blow to the government came in the mid-1980s, when U.S. firms began to close their office in the country. Congress also encouraged U.S. companies to avoid investments in South Africa.

The UDF

The United Democratic Front (UDF) formed in 1983. This new, non-racial organization was composed of 586 political, trade union, religious, student, and womens' groups — giving it a membership of more than two million people of all races. The UDF accepted the Freedom Chart and worked with the banned ANC, launching a ne widespread campaign called "Release Mandela!"

The world is watching

y now, the world watched nightly news reports
f clashes between South African police and
rotesters. Hundreds of people attended funerals
f those killed by police or white vigilantes.
wnships became ungovernable. Despite British
ime Minister Margaret Thatcher's support for the
ationalists, the Commonwealth condemned the
outh African government. Mandela's name began
ppearing in graffiti, on banners, and in songs
verywhere. In July 1988, seventy thousand people
lled Wembley Stadium in London to mark Nelson
andela's birthday in prison. The televised concert
as broadcast around the world.

Change will come

During the 1980s, the South African government
offered to release Nelson Mandela many times —
on the condition that he agreed to banishment
in the Transkei Bantustan. Each time, he refused,
but he managed to smuggle out his autobiography
while on Robben Island. In 1982, Mandela was
moved from Robben Island to Pollsmoor Prison
on the mainland in Cape Town, where he was
allowed to receive visitors. Anxious to prevent
more violence in the country, Mandela began
at last to talk to the government. These secret
meetings eventually led to his freedom.

Pollsmoor Prison

Conditions improved for Mandela, and he had fewer
restrictions at Pollsmoor. He studied for a law
degree, and also spent much time
reading and gardening.

> *"Only free men
> can negotiate;
> prisoners cannot
> enter into contracts.
> Your freedom and
> mine cannot
> be separated."*
>
> — Mandela talks about
> his frustration at being
> held prisoner

With the 1980s came
a huge increase in political
and social pressure on the
South African government to
free Nelson Mandela. Crowds
waved banners supporting the
release of the black icon at
Wembley Stadium in London
during a concert.

RELEASE *Mandela!*

In 1985, a people's march was organized from Cape Town to the
Pollsmoor prison, where Mandela was confined. The marchers' message
for Mandela was: "You have not sold the birthright of your people
to be free, and we will not rest until you are free."

STRUGGLE AGAINST APARTHEID

F. W. *de Klerk*

Born in 1936, Frederick Willem de Klerk entered parliament in 1972, and was active in the conservative wing of the National Party. When he replaced P. W. Botha as president, de Klerk presented himself as a conservative who sought only gradual reform of the apartheid system and improved diplomatic relations. No one could have guessed that de Klerk would be the president who ended apartheid.

F. W. de Klerk found it difficult to persuade the black population of South Africa to trust him.

> "Law and order must be restored ... the full power of the State has to be employed to this end."
>
> — Louis La Grange, Minister of Law and Order, justified the state of emergency declared in South Africa in 1985

In 1988, Mandela developed tuberculosis. After his hospitalization, he was moved to a cottage within Victor Verster Prison in Paarl, 31 miles (50 kilometers) outside of Cape Town, where he was allowed greater contact with friends and family.

New president

In 1985, when he was offered freedom on condition that he stop campaigning for the ANC, Mandela responded: "I cherish my own freedom, but ... I will not give any undertaking when you and I, the people, are not free." In 1989, President Botha resigned due to ill health and F. W. de Klerk was elected in his place. At first, de Klerk was no supporter of change, but eventually he realized that the country's problems would only get worse, so he began to lead South Africa in a new direction.

Historic speech

On February 2, 1990, de Klerk's opening speech to parliament did what no other South African head of state had ever done: He announced plans to begin dismantling apartheid, starting with the legalizing of the ANC and other organizations. De Klerk promised that he would release hundreds of political prisoners and suspend capital punishment. De Klerk also opened many public places — including beaches, parks, restaurants, buses, and libraries — to people of all colors.

Secret talks

Behind the scenes, Nelson Mandela held secret negotiations with the government about his release. In effect, Mandela dictated his own terms. He demanded the release of his former Robben Island comrades, including Walter Sisulu. They were finally released in October 1989. Mandela first met de Klerk in December 1989 at Tuynhuys, the official presidential office. Mandela stressed that apartheid should not just be softened but totally abandoned. De Klerk listened, but left after a disagreement with Mandela.

Surprise release

On February 10, 1990, de Klerk called Mandela to Tuynhuys again. He told Mandela that he would be released the next day!

REASONS *for change*

There were many reasons for the government's change in attitude. South Africa was increasingly isolated from the rest of the world, and trade sanctions hurt its economy. Even those countries that continued to deal with South Africa were losing patience. The ongoing state of emergency imprisoned thousands of people, yet there was still no law and order in the townships. South Africa was also fighting an undeclared war in Angola, which was proving very expensive. Even the South African army wanted things to change.

African women injured in the war between South Africa and Angola gathered for a speech.

At first Mandela refused. He wanted a week's notice to allow his family and the ANC time to prepare. But de Klerk had already informed the press, so he did not want to change the date. De Klerk also planned to fly Mandela to Johannesburg and officially release him there, but Mandela objected. Mandela wanted to walk out of the prison gates and greet the people of Cape Town. De Klerk finally consented. They sealed the deal with a glass of whiskey — but Mandela, who did not consume alcohol — only pretended to drink.

Prison guards look out from the cottage where Nelson Mandela was held prisoner. Photographers regularly attempted to get pictures of the famous prisoner.

FEBRUARY 11, 1990

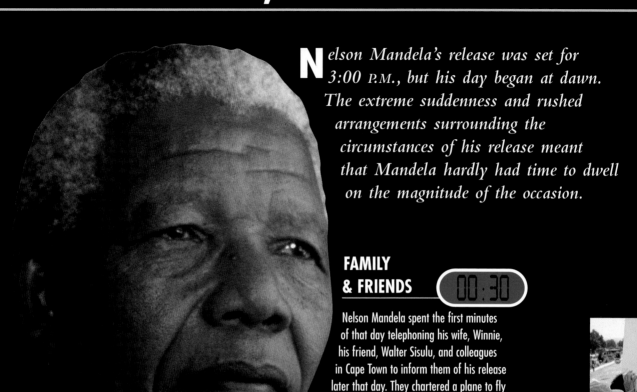

Nelson Mandela's release was set for 3:00 P.M., but his day began at dawn. The extreme suddenness and rushed arrangements surrounding the circumstances of his release meant that Mandela hardly had time to dwell on the magnitude of the occasion.

FAMILY & FRIENDS `00:30`

Nelson Mandela spent the first minutes of that day telephoning his wife, Winnie, his friend, Walter Sisulu, and colleagues in Cape Town to inform them of his release later that day. They chartered a plane to fly them to Cape Town for the historic occasion. Mandela then drafted a speech to deliver to his supporters, and finally got a few hours' sleep.

The ANC received hourly updates regarding Mandela's release.

LAST MOMENTS `04:30`

On a cloudless summer's day in Cape Town, Nelson Mandela awoke, exercised, washed, ate breakfast, and continued work on his speech. The prison doctor gave him a brief checkup, after which he telephoned colleagues at the ANC and the UDF, to request that they come to the prison to help him prepare for his release. Mandela also planned to personally say goodbye to all the prison officers.

After twenty-seven years in prison, Nelson Mandela anticipated his freedom.

VIEWPOINT

"I stood for hours on the parade in Cape Town hoping to catch a glimpse of Nelson Mandela after his historic release. Blacks and whites mingled in close proximity in a light-hearted, jovial atmosphere. The Parade was the most crowded I had ever seen it in fifteen years. Usually it was packed with cars... but on this day it was wall-to-wall people of every race you could imagine."

— bystander Andrew Malcolm

"I was at home in Cape Town. I had been waiting for this day all of my life ... now one year after graduation I found myself all alone at home watching the TV screen, trying to get a sense of history in the making. Then ... there he was — Nelson the hero, the David in our battle of apartheid .. a moment I thought I would never witness."

— South African graduate student Noel Southgate

Officials at Victor Verster Prison dealt with overwhelming press interest in Mandela's forthcoming release.

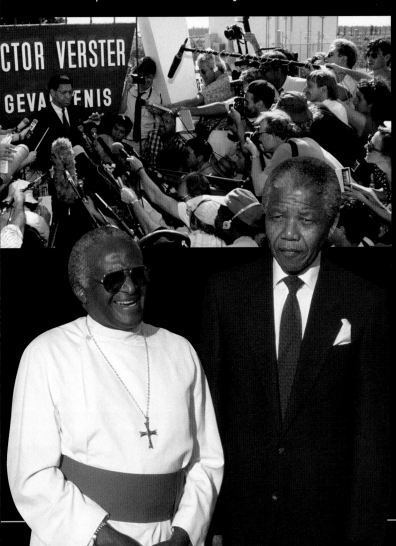

PLANS ARE MADE

Early in the morning, members of the Reception Committee, who were to oversee Mandela's release, arrived at his prison cottage. They discussed the arrangements for Mandela's appearance at the Grand Parade in Cape Town. Soon, Mandela's cottage was filled with people. Somehow he found find time during the busy preparations to pack his belongings in the boxes and crates the prison service had supplied. In his many years in prison, Mandela had accumulated enough possessions to fill over a dozen containers.

DESMOND TUTU

Mandela had not decided where to spend his first night of freedom. He wanted to stay in the black townships of Cape Town, to show his solidarity with the people. But his colleagues advised him to stay with Archbishop Desmond Tutu.

Officials advised Mandela to go to the home of Archbishop Desmond Tutu (left, in white).

FEBRUARY 11, 1990

WINNIE'S ARRIVAL `14:00`

Winnie Mandela, Walter Sisulu, and the others arrived at the cottage and sat down to a last meal prepared by Warrant Officer Swart (right), with whom Nelson Mandela had become close friends over the years. After the meal, Mandela embraced Swart and the other officers at the cottage, and began to say his farewells.

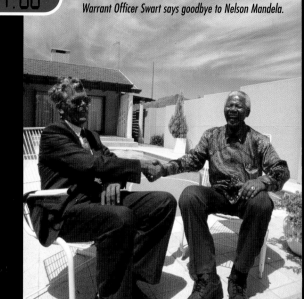

Warrant Officer Swart says goodbye to Nelson Mandela.

VIEWPOINT

The release was *"another significant step on the road to the non-racial, democratic South Africa."*

— U.S. President George H. W. Bush

LEAVING THE COTTAGE `15:55`

At 3:00 P.M., a South African TV anchorperson phoned Mandela and requested that he get out of the car just before the prison gate so they could film him walking to freedom. He agreed, but became increasingly anxious at being behind schedule. Just before 4:00 P.M., the cavalcade of cars left Mandela's cottage and stopped short of the gate. Nelson and Winnie walked the rest of the way out of prison. At the gate, Mandela saw for the first time the huge crowd of reporters and supporters. He had only expected a small group of wardens and their families!

Mandela's cavalcade stopped just short of the gate to allow Mandela to greet the crowds on foot.

CHEERS FOR MANDELA `16:00`

The crowd cheered wildly as Mandela reached the gate. Hundreds of cameras started clicking and reporters shouted questions. All the commotion flustered Nelson, and he took Winnie's hand for the last yards. When a reporter thrust a long microphone with a furry, noise-reducing cover toward him, he recoiled, thinking it was some new kind of weapon. Then Mandela raised his right fist in the ANC power salute and the crowd roared. Minutes later, Nelson Mandela climbed into another car for the drive to Cape Town.

Jubilant crowds greeted Nelson and Winnie Mandela when they walked through the Victor Verster Prison gates.

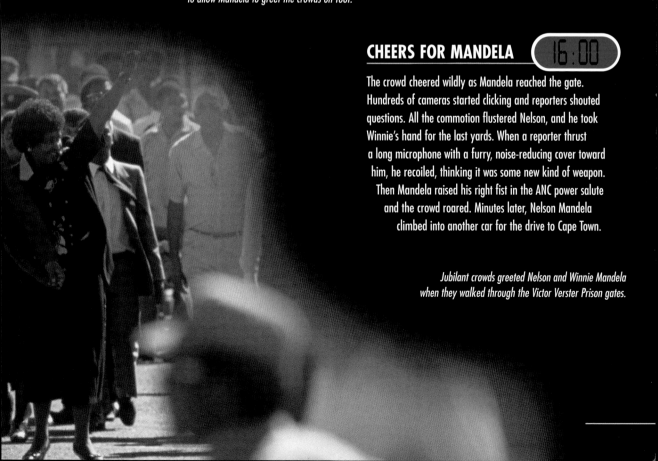

FEBRUARY 11, 1990

ON TO CAPE TOWN `16:15`

Mandela sets off for Cape Town.

As the cars drove the newly freed 71-year-old Mandela through the prosperous white farmlands, people lined the road to catch a glimpse of his motorcade. Some white people even raised their fists in the ANC salute. Mandela was so moved, he stopped and got out of the car to thank one family. While Mandela was en route to Cape Town, sixty thousand people waited with huge banners at the Grand Parade — a great open square in front of the old City Hall. Many had arrived early in the morning, and were becoming increasingly restless. Some people fainted in the heat or were injured by crowd surges. At one point, a water main burst, and people scrambled to it for handfuls of cool water.

Crowds gathered in South Africa's capital to greet Mandela.

VIEWPOINT

"The time for talking has come."
— President Kaunda of Zambia

"A triumph for national resistance and international pressure over apartheid's custodians at home and its apologists abroad."
— Sonny Ramphal (Commonwealth Secretary-General)

"Do you see how lovely the people of South Africa can be?"
— Young man at the Cape Town City Hall

"We are one nation, black and white. We are one people."
— Old man at the Cape Town City Hall

OUT OF CONTROL?   `16:30`

Meanwhile, in the backstreets around the Grand Parade, police opened fire at groups of youths, who the officers claimed were smashing windows and looting shops. The police also fired pellets and rubber bullets to disperse sections of the crowd. Mobile medical units treated the injured, including children, who were lying on stretchers. In other parts of the country, crowds celebrating Mandela's release were also attacked by police.

Several riots took place the day of Mandela's release.

GRAND PARADE

By the time Mandela reached the outskirts of Cape Town, the immensity of the welcoming rally became apparent. Hordes of people streamed towards the Grand Parade. Mandela's driver at first hoped to take his important passenger through the crowd, but turned back when a huge crowd surrounded the car, knocking on the windows, jumping on the top, and rocking it. The driver began to panic, so Mandela suggested they calm down at the house of his friend and attorney, Dullah Omar. After refreshing drinks, they drove to the rear entrance of the Grand Parade.

FEBRUARY 11, 1990

Reverend Allan Boesak urged the crowd to be patient.

WAITING

It was dusk when Nelson Mandela eventually addressed the crowds at the Grand Parade. Two anti-apartheid clerics, the Reverend Frank Chicane and the Reverend Allan Boesak, had urged patience as the hours passed. Although many of the original sixty thousand dispersed, about ten thousand people remained. Similar crowds gathered at towns and cities throughout the country. Revelers filled the centers of Johannesburg and Soweto, which were normally quiet on a Sunday. Mandela's speech was broadcast live around the world.

Mandela's supporters eagerly awaited his famous speech.

MANDELA IS READY

Mandela walked through the back entrance of the City Hall and up to the top floor. When he walked out onto the balcony, the crowd cheered and clapped, raising flags and banners above their heads. Cheering and chanting grew louder as Mandela raised his fist into the air. He took out the speech he had written only hours earlier, but when he reached into his pocket for his glasses, Mandela realized he had left them in prison. He had to borrow Winnie's glasses to read the speech!

Nelson Mandela delivered his speech to a crowd of more than 10,000 people.

THE SPEECH STARTS

In his speech, Mandela thanked all the people across the globe that had campaigned for his release, reserving special thanks for all the anti-apartheid organizations in South Africa itself. He also acknowledged his family, whose pain and suffering, he believed, "was far greater than my own." He was careful to tell people that he had not made any deals with the government for his release. Then he praised de Klerk, but warned that the fight against apartheid was not yet over. "The sight of freedom looming on the horizon should encourage us to redouble our efforts," he said.

PHONE CALLS FROM OLD FRIENDS

After his speech, Mandela was hustled back into a car and driven away. Even now, black faces lined the streets, singing and calling his name. That evening he stayed at the house of Archbishop Desmond Tutu, where he was met by his family and friends. During the evening, he had a phone call that was very important to him: his old friend, Oliver Tambo, spoke to him from Stockholm, Sweden, where he was recovering from a stroke.

Mandela spent his first night of freedom in the home of Archbishop Desmond Tutu.

VIEWPOINT

"*I stand here before you not as a prophet, but as a humble servant of you, the people.*"

"*I have fought against white domination and I have fought against black domination. I have cherished the ideal of a democratic and free society in which all peoples live together in harmony and with equal opportunity. It is an ideal which I hope to live for and to achieve, but if needs be, it is an ideal for which I am prepared to die.*"

— quotes from Mandela's speech

A NATIONAL HERO

The day after his release, the real work for Nelson Mandela and the ANC began. Apartheid was still in place and so was the government that had upheld it for so long at such great cost to millions of South African lives. Mandela embarked on a punishing schedule of meetings, working hard to negotiate a new constitution, and helping the ANC become a proper political party.

Foreign travels

In June 1990, Mandela went on a six-week tour of Europe and North America to meet with world leaders. In Paris, he met President Mitterand. He traveled through Switzerland, Italy, the Netherlands, and England. On his arrival in New York, he was greeted by a ticker-tape parade through the streets, which were crowded with more than one million people. Mandela met President George H. W. Bush, urging him not to halt sanctions until apartheid was completely destroyed and an interim government was in place. Before his return to South Africa, Mandela also made trips to the African countries of Uganda, Kenya, and Mozambique.

Limited progress

Shortly after Mandela's release, the government signed an agreement with the ANC to repeal repressive laws, release political prisoners and continue negotiating. Yet the violence in the countr continued, and more than three thousand people were killed in 1990 alone. Mandela was eager

Mandela inspects the troops during his visit to Britain.

INKATHA

Inkatha is a political organization formed in 1975 by Chief Gatsha Buthelezi (right). It is named after the strong headgear worn by Zulu women to carry heavy loads. Buthelezi is the leader of six million Zulus, the biggest ethnic group in South Africa. Although its aims were to create a non-racial democratic system in South Africa, Inkatha had tried to work with the white government, which led to criticism from the ANC.

o speed up the process of dismantling apartheid and rebuilding the country. He persuaded the ANC o suspend the armed struggle in order to show good aith. A month later the government lifted the state f emergency. However, it became clear to many that le Klerk still had race-based prejudices.

Inkatha

One serious problem was the violence in Natal, where Chief Buthelezi's conservative Inkatha movement had declared war on the ANC and was burning entire villages down, killing many people. Mandela and others began to suspect that the conflict was being fueled by the South African police, and was backed by the government in order to discredit African movements. Mandela visited Inkatha leaders, telling them: "take your guns, your knives, and your pangas, and throw them into the sea!"

ANC conference

In July 1991, the ANC held its first conference in Johannesburg in thirty years. More than 2,200 delegates attended. Mandela was elected president of the ANC, and talk turned to transforming an illegal underground liberation movement into a legal mass political party. As Mandela said in his speech, "The struggle is not over."

A NATIONAL HERO

Nelson Mandela and F. W. de Klerk show off their Nobel Peace Prizes.

Negotiations

At the end of 1991, the Convention for a Democratic South Africa (CODESA) was held in Johannesburg. Representatives from eighteen organizations met to negotiate a new constitution, but each party had a different agenda and the talks failed. A whites-only referendum in May 1992 showed that two-thirds favored negotiations, which prompted a new round of talks. CODESA II, however, also failed to make a breakthrough. It was not until the next year that the ANC and the government agreed on what they should do. They decided that a five-year government of national unity, made up of representatives from all the political parties, would write the new constitution for the country. A date was set for the election: April 27, 1994.

Tragedies

Meanwhile, the new South Africa experienced a wave of violence. In June 1992, Inkatha supporters shot or hacked to death forty-nine men, women, and children in a black settlement called Boipatong. Witnesses claimed they saw Inkatha people brought in on police trucks. The ANC broke off talks with the government in protest until de Klerk called a halt to the violence. Then, just months later, the popular black activist Chris Hani was shot dead in front of his house by a member of a white-supremacist group. The assassination led to mass rioting. Mandela begged the people to stay calm and peaceful in order to maintain the progress toward majority rule.

The election

Despite the violence, election plans were not disrupted. Black voters — many of whom would be voting for the first time in their lives —

NOBEL *prize*

In 1993, Mandela and F. W. de Klerk were both awarded the Nobel Peace Prize and traveled to Oslo, Norway, to receive it. "Five years ago, people would have seriously questioned the sanity of anyone who predicted that Mr. Mandela and I would be joint recipients of the 1993 Nobel Peace Prize," de Klerk said in his Nobel lecture. "And yet both of us are here before you today."

DIVORCE *from Winnie*

After leaving prison, Nelson Mandela had little time to spend with his family. In 1992, his marriage to Winnie broke up. Winnie had been convicted on a kidnapping charge stemming from the abduction of a fourteen-year-old boy who was later found beaten to death. Mandela stood by Winnie during the trial, but eventually acknowledged that the marriage was over.

nd many of whom were illiterate) needed to educated. On the day of the election, twenty-ree million people lined up patiently to cast their tes. The mood in the country became more sitive and the violence ceased. The ANC won the election with about two-thirds of the vote. Nelson Mandela became South Africa's first black president.

Nelson and Winnie Mandela divorced in 1992.

Millions of black voters waited patiently for hours to vote for the first time.

A NATIONAL HERO

NEW *home*

After his release, Mandela built a house in Qunu, in the Transkei, where he was born. On the grounds, he also built an exact replica of the warden's cottage in which he was held at Victor Verster Prison. Every year, he hosts a Christmas party there, attended by thousands of children and parents.

President Mandela

After the election, world leaders came to South Africa to pay tribute to Mandela. However, after the celebrations, Mandela faced innumerable tasks. The new ANC-led government inherited a country in economic decline, with widespread corruption and racial division. Mandela committed himself to eradicating the extensive and damaging repercussions of the apartheid system — in particular, the inequality between blacks and whites. But he also needed to maintain a growing economy that could provide jobs for everyone. Change was slow. Many Africans stayed poor, and violent protests broke out around the country.

New government

Mandela's government included African, Indian, and white ministers, and even some former supporters of apartheid. Many of these ministers were inexperienced, and Mandela frequently took matters into his own hands as the quickest way to get things done, despite the ANC's long history of collective decision-making. He allocated 4.2 billion rand (about $6 million

U.S. dollars) to reform health, housing, and educational systems, and to promote economic growth. He promised, among other things, to buil three hundred thousand new homes a year by the turn of the century. Mandela also passed the Restitution of Land Rights Act, which returned lan taken from blacks under apartheid.

New constitution

While it took almost two years to wri South Africa's new constitutio what resulted was one of the most ambitious

Nelson Mandela meets President Bill Clinton, who became a close personal friend of the new South African president.

nstitutions in the world. On the day in 1996 hen it was passed, delegates and spectators the parliament chamber broke out spontaneously to jubilant celebrations. "This is the day when uth Africa is truly born," said Cyril Ramaphosa, airman of the assembly. The constitution outlawed scrimination on the basis of race, gender, sexual ientation, age, pregnancy, or marital status. It so granted its citizens rights to adequate housing, od, water, health care, education, and social curity — all of which were withheld from the ack majority during the apartheid era.

Truth and Reconciliation Commission

1996, the Truth and Reconciliation Commission as established to investigate the political crimes the apartheid era. Archbishop Desmond Tutu aired the Commission, which spent more than o years compiling its report, and which included ore than twenty thousand statements from dividual victims of human rights abuses. The goal as not to punish the perpetrators, but to ask for blic apologies. Mandela said, "If we don't forgive em, then that feeling of bitterness and revenge ll always be there."

Commission findings

any people were called before the Commission, cluding F. W. de Klerk, who begged forgiveness r the apartheid years, and Winnie Mandela, ho was questioned about the violent behavior f her bodyguards. The Commission condemned e human rights abuses of the apartheid state, ccusing President Botha of involvement in many f the atrocities. In 1998, the Commission published report, in spite of a last-minute attempt by e Klerk to have his name removed in connection apartheid-era injustices. Many black South ricans felt that the Commission let a great mber of guilty people off too easily. They also lieved that apologies alone were not enough.

Sports supporter

Mandela chose a powerful means to bridge the racial gap: sport. As president, he made public appearances at important rugby matches — traditionally a game played only by white South Africans. He was present at the final of the Rugby World Cup in 1995 and, when South

Mandela regularly appeared in front of huge sporting crowds wearing the traditional colors of South African teams.

Africa beat New Zealand, he presented the trophy to the South African captain, François Pienaar, dressed in the green springbok jersey. Mandela was also fundamental in luring the Cricket World Cup to South Africa in 2003 and appeared in television ads promoting the event.

SYMBOL OF FREEDOM

As president, Nelson Mandela became a great ambassador for his country and a symbol of freedom and humanity everywhere. Every year, he received about five thousand requests for appearances and official engagements, of which he could only accept a small proportion. Even so, his calendar was booked for months ahead, with nearly every hour of every day planned out. Archbishop Desmond Tutu said, "He leaves me panting in exhaustion just looking at the schedule he keeps."

After retirement from the political arena, Nelson Mandela continued his public appearances — such as this one with the Spice Girls.

Diplomat

Mandela's great talents for compassion, humor, and political shrewdness allowed him to maintain relations with leaders from all ends of the political spectrum, from U.S. presidents to Cuban leader Fidel Castro. He also kept diplomatic ties with Colonel Muammar al-Qaddafi and Yasir Arafat, men seen as dangerous extremists by the U.S. Mandela remembered that these men helped the ANC during its long fight against apartheid.

Remarriage

In his seventies, Mandela met and became close friends with Grace Machel, the widow of the former leader of Mozambique. She, like Mandela, has long campaigned for human rights, in particular for women and children. In 1998, on his eightieth birthday, Mandela married Grace, saying of her, "She is my life." Between them, they have forty-five children and grandchildren, with whom Nelso spends as much time as possible.

Charity work

In 1995, Mandela founded The Nelson Mandela Children's Fund with a personal contribution of thirty percent of his salary. Since then, the charity has raised more than $33 million in U.S. dollars and distributed approximately $10 million into its projects to alleviate child poverty. In recent years, the Children's Fund has

...ifted its focus to children and families affected by ...e spread of HIV and AIDS.

AIDS epidemic

...our million people in South Africa are HIV-positive. ...n average, six hundred people a day die from ...DS-related illnesses and more than 660,000 ...ildren have lost both their parents to HIV and ...DS. Part of the problem has been the reluctance ...f South African leaders to talk about an issue that ...any Africans feel is "private." When he was president, Mandela feared upsetting voters by talking about the disease. Since his retirement, however, Mandela has campaigned relentlessly on the issue and raised much-needed funds. Current president Thabo Mbeki

AID *for AIDS*

A breakthrough in the fight against AIDS occurred in 1991 when a group of thirty-nine multinational pharmaceutical companies dropped their battle to stop South Africa from importing cheap, generic AIDS drugs.

Campaigners in South Africa work to raise awareness about AIDS. This, combined with greater access to new drugs to combat the virus, means more hope for South Africa in the future.

Mandela married Grace Machel on his eightieth birthday.

Although retired, Mandela travels extensively to fulfill his duties. Here he talks with the Secretary General of the United Nations, Kofi Annan (above, right).

Nelson Mandela handpicked Thabo Mbeki (above), as his Deputy President. In 1999, Mbeki succeeded Mandela as president of South Africa.

has also proved reluctant to speak on the issue and has even expressed doubts about the extent to which the AIDS virus has spread in South Africa.

Retirement

In 1999, after five years as president, Mandela retired and returned to his home in the Transkei where he had been born. Yet he still travels and meets world leaders and is one of the world's most famous and inspirational men, celebrated everywhere. His views on world events — from strife in his own country to the war in Iraq — continues to command attention. Today, Mandela jokes about when he will retire from retirement!

Successor

Mandela's deputy, Thabo Mbeki, succeeded him as president. A long-term anti-apartheid activist, Mbeki spent many years in exile in Britain and the Soviet Union, where he trained as a guerrilla fighter. Acutely aware of the difficulty of filling Mandela's shoes as president, he has focused

on raising living standards for the black population and making sure the economy flourishes.

Health scare

Despite the fact that Nelson Mandela is in his eighties and can appear fragile, he is remarkably fit and generally healthy. He travels everywhere with his own doctor. In July 2001, however, Mandela was diagnosed as having prostate cancer, and underwent seven months of radiation treatments in Cape Town. "I am going to stay on top of this little development," he said with typical understatement and humor. In February 2002, he announced that the treatments were successful.

WINNIE'S *future*

In 2003, Winnie Mandela was in court again, this time on charges of fraud and theft. She was sentenced to five years in prison. Like a modern-day Robin Hood, she was convicted of fraudulently acquiring loans for people who were desperately poor. Winnie remains a controversial figure — but one who commands great respect among many people of South Africa.

> *"If any man on earth has earned the right to speak his mind, then Mandela has."*
>
> — *Bill Clinton*

Art for charity

In 2002, Mandela turned his hand to another skill — painting. He produced a series of colorful charcoal and pastel drawings inspired by his time on Robben Island, and sold them to raise money for his children's charity. The drawings went on display in London, and on Robben Island, which is now South Africa's first World Heritage Site. Part of the Site is now named in honor of its most famous prisoner — Nelson Mandela.

Mandela movie

Production began in 2003 on *Long Walk To Freedom*, a movie based on Nelson Mandela's life, featuring Morgan Freeman in the starring role. Freeman said, "I am honored and terrified that I won't live up to the job of really presenting this man."

> *"Give us, the people, the chance freely to determine the future of our country!"*
>
> — *Thabo Mbeki speaking upon his election as the new President of South Africa*

Morgan Freeman (left) has played many characters throughout his acting career, but his starring role in the movie of Long Walk to Freedom (based on Nelson Mandela's autobiography) may prove the most important and challenging of his life. The film's British director, Shekhar Kapur, said, "Mandela is a spiritual leader like Gandhi."

FUTURE CHALLENGES

South Africa faces many tough challenges in the future. Even with apartheid dismantled, the bulk of the economy, including most of the land, remains mainly white-owned, with many of the best jobs going to whites. Poverty and inequality continue to be major issues, and murder rates are ten times higher than in the United States.

Ongoing battle

The spread of AIDS is South Africa's most serious problem today. One in nine people is infected with HIV and more than 150 HIV-positive children are born daily. In 2002, the Nelson Mandela Children's Fund joined forces with the Diana, Princess of Wales Memorial Fund to launch a massive support effort for children and families affected by the crisis. When she visited, just five months before she died in 1997, Diana and Mandela had planned a joint fund drive. After her death, Mandela praised Diana's commitment to humanitarian causes, saying, "Her inspiration must continue to change lives now and in the future."

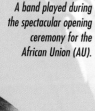

A band played during the spectacular opening ceremony for the African Union (AU).

NGO *networks*

Non-governmental Organizations (NGOs) have created a vast network of organizations in South Africa to help combat the spread of AIDS. The National Association for People With Aids (NAPWA) has become a powerful voice for those living with the virus. In February 2000, the government launched the National AIDS Council (NAC) made up of representatives from the government, business, NGOs and the medical sector.

Members of this young family are infected with the AIDS virus.

Powerful party

Some people fear that the ANC is becoming too powerful. Its aim to achieve a two-thirds majority in a national election would allow it to make sweeping changes without consulting any of the other political parties. It also wants to change the clause in the constitution so that a president can serve more than the maximum two terms that are allowed by the present constitution. Some people worry that the other parties in South African politics are already too weak to provide an effective opposition and that this could damage democracy.

Brain drain

South Africa also faces the challenge of finding ways to encourage its skilled professional workers to stay in the country. Thousands emigrate every year in search of a better life. Many leave because of the high levels of crime, rising unemployment, and fear of the AIDS epidemic. The government is hoping to reverse this trend, giving financial and business support to companies that are training black workers to fill the gaps. Other people, however, believe that the government should find ways to encourage immigration to South Africa from other countries.

The African Union

In 2002, the African Union (AU) was established. At its inauguration, it was made up of fifty-three African countries from all over the continent. South African president Thabo Mbeki is its first chairman. Based loosely on its northern counterpart, the European Union (EU), the AU's aims to encourage the spread of democracy throughout Africa.

"That was one of the things that worried me — to be raised to the position of a semi-god — because then you are no longer a human being. I wanted to be known as Mandela, a man with weaknesses, some of which are fundamental, and a man who is committed, but nevertheless, sometimes he fails to live up to expectations."

— *Nelson Mandela*

TIME LINE

1400–1799

- 1488: Portuguese explorer Bartholomeu Diaz becomes the first European to sail around the tip of South Africa.

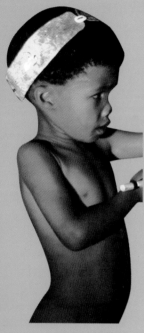

- 1600s: Bantu-speaking peoples move into the region that is modern-day South Africa, including the Sotho, Swazi, Zulu, and Xhosa (Mandela's people).

- 1652: Dutch settlers establish Cape Town on the very tip of southern Africa to act as a port-of-call for traders traveling from Europe to the Far East.

- 1795: The British invade Cape Town and temporarily seize the colony from the Dutch.

1800–1899

- 1806: The British attempt to occupy Cape Town for the second time.

- 1814: The British purchase Cape Town and the surrounding area for about 10 million U.S. dollars

- 1836–1856: The Dutch, wishing to escape British rule, found the republics of Transvaal, the Orange Free State, and Cape Colony.

- 1867: Large reserves of diamonds are discovered at Kimberley, Cape Colony.

- 1886: Gold is discovered in the Transvaal. This, together with the earlier diamond find, encourages a rush of European prospectors, who come into conflict with the Boers (Dutch farmers).

- 1899–1902: Anglo-Boer War results in the Boers surrendering control of the Transvaal and its diamond and gold mines to Britain.

1900–1919

- 1910: The Union of South Africa is formed, comprising the Cape of Good Hope, Natal, Orange Free State, and Transvaal.

- 1910: Pass laws require black people to carry travel, work, residential, and curfew passes. Blacks were punished for not producing them when requested.

- 1911: New laws bar blacks from working in many types of occupation.

- 1912: The first national association for black people, the South African Native National Congress (SANNC), is founded.

- 1913: The Native Land Act makes it illegal for blacks to own land except in a few native reserves that cover just over seven percent of the total land.

- 1914: General J. B. M. Herzog founds the National Party to promote Afrikaner interests.

- 1914–18: World War I is fought.

- July 18, 1918: Nelson Mandela is born.

1920–1952

- 1923: The South African government passes the Urban Areas Act and creates certain areas — usually located on the outskirts of cities — where ma blacks are forced to live.

- 1923: The South African Nati National Congress (SANNC), which was founded in 1912, changes its name to the African National Congress (ANC).

- 1924: Certain unskilled jobs are restricted to white applicants only.

- 1933: The United Party, formed when the Nationalist Party joined forces with the opposition South African Party, comes to power in the South African government.

- 1944: Nelson Mandela, Olive Tambo, Walter Sisulu, and several others form the ANC Youth League, which has a mor radical agenda than the ANC.

- 1944: Nelson Mandela marrie his first wife, Evelyn Mase. (They divorce in 1958.)

- March 1950: Mandela joins the ANC National Executive.

- 1952: the Defiance Campaign is started, which plans to use massive civil disobedience to render apartheid unworkable.

952–1959

952: Mandela is elected
sident of the ANC Youth
gue and deputy president
he ANC itself.

Mandela opens a law practice
ohannesburg with his friend
er Tambo as partner.

954–1955: The Congress
he People, composed of
-apartheid organizations
oughout South Africa,
ws up the Freedom Charter
ing for equality for all.
son Mandela is one of
organizers.

956: Mandela and other
ck activists are arrested
d tried for high treason.
se Treason
ls last
il 1961,
n all the
used are
uitted.

958: Mandela marries
mzamo Winifred Madikizela,
o becomes popularly known
Winnie Mandela.

1960–1969

• March 1960: The Sharpeville
Massacre occurs, in which sixty-
nine blacks protesting the Pass
laws are killed by police, with
many more injured, making
headlines worldwide. The trouble
resulting from this incident leads
the government to ban the ANC.

• 1961: Mandela becomes
Commander in Chief of Umkhonto
we Sizwe ("Spear of the Nation"),
the military wing of the ANC.

• August 1962: Mandela is
arrested and later sentenced to six
years' imprisonment on Robben
Island, off the coast of Cape Town.

• October 1963: Mandela is
charged with sabotage at the
famous Rivonia Trial.

• June 1964: Mandela is
sentenced to life imprisonment
in Robben Island Prison.

1970–1989

• 1976: The Soweto Massacre —
police kill more than five hundred
unarmed students protesting against
apartheid.

• 1977: Black activist Steve Biko
is arrested and is murdered twenty-
six days later in prison.

• 1982: Mandela is moved from
Robben Island Prison to Pollsmoor
Prison in Cape Town.

• 1985: Mandela is offered
freedom on the condition that
he renounces political violence.
He refuses the offer.

• 1987: Mandela begins secret
talks with the government.

• 1988: Mandela is moved into
a private cottage on the grounds
of Victor Verster Prison in Paarl.

• October 1989: Mandela's former
Robben Island comrades, including
Walter Sisulu,
are released.

• 1989: Mandela
meets President
F. W. de Klerk.
This meeting
is followed by
others, after
which de Klerk
eventually agrees
to Mandela's
unconditional
release.

1990–1999

• 1990: the South African
government announces the
acceptance of the ANC and the
release of many political prisoners.

• February 11, 1990: Nelson
Mandela is released from prison
after ten thousand days.

• July 1990: Mandela is elected
president of the ANC.

• 1993: Nelson Mandela and
F. W. de Klerk are awarded
the Nobel Peace Prize.

• 10 May, 1994: Mandela is elected
president of South Africa in the
country's first elections in which
everyone can vote.

• 1996: The Truth and
Reconciliation Commission is formed
to investigate the political
crimes of the apartheid era.

• 1998: Mandela divorces Winnie
Mandela and marries Grace Machel.

• June 1999: Mandela retires
from public life at the end
of his five-year presidential term.

GLOSSARY

activist someone who devotes time and energy to a political or social cause.

Afrikaans an official language of the Republic of South Africa, closely related to Dutch and Flemish.

Afrikaner an inhabitant of the Republic of South Africa who speaks Afrikaans and is descended from the original Dutch or Huguenot settlers.

ambassador a representative of a country; informal ambassadors who represent their country through their reputation and deeds.

apartheid the enforced separation of African, European, and Indian people in South Africa.

Bantu a group of similar languages spoken widely in southern, eastern and central Africa, including Zulu, Swahili, and Xhosa; also the name of people who speak any of these languages. The word "Bantu" means "people" in Zulu.

Bantustans areas in South Africa where non-whites were forced by the authorities to live under apartheid.

Boer South Africans descended from the original Dutch or Huguenot settlers; now referred to as Afrikaners.

boycott to protest against a person, organization, or country by refusing to deal with it or buy products from it.

civil disobedience legal actions such as marches and demonstrations that protest against unfair laws.

colony a country or region that is being ruled by another country.

colored term used in South Africa to describe people of a mixed white and black genetic background.

communist a supporter of a political system in which the government controls all property and industries.

conservative an individual or organization that favors the preservation of established customs or values, and opposes change.

constitution a written document that states the aims of a country or organization and sets out how it will be run.

democratic description of a form of political system in a country in which everyone has equal rights.

detention the confinement of a person awaiting trial.

dissent in political terms, the expression of disagreement with a prevailing view or political system.

exile a prolonged, usually enforced, absence from your own country.

ghetto a densely populated part of a city where the poorest people, often of the same racial or ethnic background, live.

guerilla term used to describe small-scale, often politically motivated warfare, usually to combat a larger force such as the army or police. Rather than confronting a much larger enemy out in the open, guerrillas attack and destroy infrastructure, such as power supplies and transportation links.

house arrest forced confinement, usually in one's own house. Many political activists have been kept under house arrest in countries around the world to prevent them from creating unrest. House arrest was a common practice in South Africa under apartheid.

human rights the rights of individuals to freedom and justice.

Inkatha a Zulu political organization formed in 1975 by Chief Gatsha Buthelezi, which aimed to create a non-racial democratic system in South Africa, but which worked with the white government. Following Nelson Mandela's release, supporters of Inkatha and the ANC were involved in a series of violent clashes that many felt were stirred up by the white government.

legislation the process of making a law, or the law itself.

migration the movement and settlement of people from one place, region, or country to another.

negotiations peaceful discussions to solve a dispute.

nomad a person who moves from place to place to find food and land for animals to graze.

panga an African Machete with a broad blade.

petition a letter signed by many people requesting that a government or organization do or change something.

radical someone who favors extreme or fundamental changes to a political, economic or social system.

reconciliation the coming together of opposing groups to settle their differences.

sabotage the deliberate damage or destruction of equipment or machinery for political reasons.

sanctions measures taken by one country against another to attempt to force a change of policy. Sanctions usually take the form of suspending trade with another country, refusing to buy their goods, or to supply them with goods manufactured in any other country.

segregation the practice of creating separate facilities within the same society. For example, apartheid in South Africa meant separate facilities for whites and blacks.

state of emergency a period during which a government withdraws rights, such as freedom of speech, in order to limit the possibility of mass violence. A state of emergency is also accompanied by restrictions on movement, such as a curfew during the hours of darkness.

strike a form of protest in which people show their unhappiness with conditions by stopping their regular action — such as working, eating, or buying goods — until the situation improves.

township an area such as a town or city where blacks had to live under apartheid. One such township, Soweto, was the site of the massacre of over five hundred protesting students by the South African police in 1976.

treason the crime of attempting to act against, damage, or overthrow the government of a country.

United Nations an international organization formed in New York City in 1945 to represent all the governments of the world and to promote peace, cooperation and security between them.

vigilante a person who takes upon him or herself the protection of his or her district or property.

white supremacy a theory or belief that white people are naturally superior to people of other races.

FURTHER INFORMATION

Books

Apartheid in South Africa. Troubled World (series). Sean Connolly (Raintree/Steck Vaughn)

Biko. Donald Woods (Henry Holt & Company)

The End of Apartheid: A New South Africa. Point of Impact (series). Richard Tames (Heinemann Library)

Long Walk to Freedom: The Autobiography of Nelson Mandela. Nelson Mandela (Little, Brown & Company)

Nelson Mandela. Trailblazers of the Modern World (series). Gini Holland (World Almanac Library)

Nelson Mandela: Activist for Equality. Journey to Freedom (series). Robert Green (Childs World)

Nelson Mandela: An Unauthorized Biography. Heinemann Profiles (series). Sean Connolly (Heinemann Library)

Nelson Mandela. Breaking Barriers Set I (series). Jill C. Wheeler (Abdo & Daughters)

Nelson Mandela: Father of Freedom. Famous Lives (series). Hakim Adi (Raintree/Steck Vaughn)

Nelson Mandela. Leading Lives (series). Liz Gogerly (Heinemann Library)

Nelson Mandela. Twentieth Century History Makers. (series). Ann Kramer (Raintree/Steck Vaughn)

The Release of Nelson Mandela. Dates With History (series). John Malam (Smart Apple Media)

Web Sites

www.anc.org.za/index.html Connect with this web site for the African National Congress and related links.

www.africanhistory.about.com/library/biographies/blbio-stevebiko.htm Learn about famous black martyr, Steve Biko.

www.safrica.info/ess_info/sa_glance/history/apartmuseum.htm Take a virtual tour of what the apartheid museum has to offer.

www.angelfire.com/ak3/apartheid/apartheid.html Read a quick history of apartheid.

www.robben-island.org.za/departments/heritage/gallery/mandela.asp Discover what Mandela's life was like at Robben Island Prison.

travel.guardian.co.uk/print/0,3858,4586315-104895,00.html Relive Mandela's last fourteen months of prison at Victor Verster Prison.

www.sbf.org.za/ Visit the Steve Biko Foundation web site.

INDEX